~

$\mathcal{T}$o: _____

$\mathcal{F}$rom: _____

$\mathcal{D}$ate: _____

~

THE MIRROR

Our Children See

THE MIRROR OUR CHILDREN SEE

Library of Congress Cataloging-in-Publication Data:
The mirror our children see.
p.   cm.
ISBN 0-8499-5159-3
1. Christian life—Quotations, maxims, etc. 2. Bible—Quotations.
3. Parenting—Religious aspects—Christianity. I. Word Publishing.
BV4513.M57   1995
242'.645—dc20
95-19170
CIP

THE MIRROR

Our Children See

WORD PUBLISHING
Dallas • London • Vancouver • Melbourne

$\mathcal{Y}$ou should be able to tell your children to do as you do, not just as you say.

~

For I have given you an example, that you should do as I have done to you.

JOHN 13:15

If your kids live for Jesus now,

they won't have a lot of regrets later.

~

Remember now your Creator in the days of your youth,
before the difficult days come, and the years draw near
when you say, "I have no pleasure in them."

ECCLESIASTES 12:1

$\mathcal{W}$hen you feel like blowing up at
your kids, remind yourself how long
Jesus has put up with you.

~

However, for this reason I obtained mercy, that in me first
Jesus Christ might show all longsuffering, as a pattern to those
who are going to believe on Him for everlasting life.

1 TIMOTHY 1:16

*Y*our son or daughter can have an
awesome impact for Christ at home, school,
or church. So can you.

~

*Let no one despise your youth, but be an
example to the believers in word, in conduct,
in love, in spirit, in faith, in purity.*

1 Timothy 4:12

$\mathcal{S}$acrificing for your kids is a glorious calling.

Jesus did it for you.

~

For to this you were called, because
Christ also suffered for us, leaving us an example,
that you should follow His steps.

1 PETER 2:21

If you work on developing character in

your children, God will take care

of their reputation.

~

Even a child is known by his deeds, whether what
he does is pure and right.

6

$\mathcal{D}$oes the way you live give God pleasure?
If you do His will, it will. Being a good
parent is part of His will.

~

The steps of a good man are ordered by the LORD,
and He delights in his way.

PSALM 37:23

7

*T*he most important inheritance
you will leave your children is not
money but godly parents.

~

*Riches do not profit in the day of wrath, but
righteousness delivers from death.*

PROVERBS 11:4

God calls us as parents to shepherd
our own little flock with integrity and skill.

~

So he shepherded them according to the integrity of his heart, and guided them by the skillfulness of his hands.

PSALM 78:72

$\mathcal{J}$ust as God wants us to look to
Him for guidance, so our children
should be able to look to us.

~

Will you not from this time cry to Me, "My Father,
You are the guide of my youth?"

JEREMIAH 3:4

Every day and in every way,

our children should be taught

the Word of God.

~

That from childhood you have
known the Holy Scriptures, which are
able to make you wise for salvation through
faith which is in Christ Jesus.

2 TIMOTHY 3:15

Our efforts to train our children are never wasted. Sooner or later, they will come around.

~

Train up a child in the way he should go, and when he is old he will not depart from it.

PROVERBS 22:6

The heritage you and I give to our children and grandchildren is the most important contribution we can make to their lives.

~

Children's children are the crown of old men, and the glory of children is their father.

PROVERBS 17:6

$\mathcal{W}$e know God is doing a work in our hearts when we are burdened for our children's spiritual welfare, and they for ours.

~

And he will turn the hearts of the fathers to the children, and the hearts of the children to their fathers....

MALACHI 4:6

$\mathcal{W}$e need to show

compassion and for

as God shows us.

~

As a father pities his children, so the LORD
pities those who fear Him.

PSALM 103:13

$\mathcal{W}$e should be bold as we
instruct our children in godly living.

~

As you know how we exhorted, and comforted,
and charged every one of you, as a father
does his own children.

1 Thessalonians 2:11

$\mathcal{P}$arents who love their children and
care how they turn out will discipline them.
And children know this.

~

He who spares his rod hates his son, but he
who loves him disciplines him promptly.

PROVERBS 13:24

*W*hat an awesome opportunity we have
as parents to build our children's confidence
in their heavenly Father!

~

*If you then, being evil, know how to give good gifts to
your children, how much more will your Father who is
in heaven give good things to those who ask Him!*

MATTHEW 7:11

The more we hide God's Word in our hearts, the more likely it will be on our lips whenever and wherever we are with our kids.

~

And these words which I command you today shall be in your heart. You shall teach them diligently to your children, and shall talk of them when you sit in your house, when you walk by the way, when you lie down, and when you rise up.

DEUTERONOMY 6:6–7

*I*nstead of complaining
about how much our children
cost us, we should thank God we have
them to spend our money on.

~

*... For the children ought not to lay up for the parents,
but the parents for the children.*

2 CORINTHIANS 12:14

$\mathcal{G}$od provides for all of our needs,

and we as parents have the privilege of

doing the same for our family.

~

*But if anyone does not provide for his own, and
especially for those of his household, he has denied
the faith and is worse than an unbeliever.*

1 TIMOTHY 5:8

The more time we spend training
our children on the front end, the less time
we will have to spend disciplining them
on the back end.

~

And you, fathers, do not provoke your children
to wrath, but bring them up in the training
and admonition of the Lord.

EPHESIANS 6:4

22

The best way to give your children security is to show them that Dad loves Mom and Mom loves Dad—and that they have mutual respect for each other.

~

Husbands, love your wives, just as Christ also loved the church and gave Himself for her.

EPHESIANS 5:25

$\mathcal{O}$ur children not only respect us when
we discipline them correctly and in love, but
they also learn how to love and submit
to their heavenly Father.

~

*We have had human fathers who corrected us, and
we paid them respect. Shall we not much more readily
be in subjection to the Father of spirits and live?*

HEBREWS 12:9

$\mathcal{W}$e understand the heart of
God when we see our families as the
greatest blessing in this life.

~

*Your wife shall be like a fruitful vine in
the very heart of your house, your children like
olive plants all around your table.*

PSALM 128:3

As with the prodigal, we pray that our kids
will come to their senses when they experience
the consequences of their own choices.

~

*But when he came to himself, he said, "How
many of my father's hired servants have bread enough
and to spare, and I perish with hunger!"*

LUKE 15:17

Children learn self-control through parental guidance, not by having their own way.

~

It is good for a man to bear the yoke in his youth.

LAMENTATIONS 3:27

When a mom or dad leaves the family,

God can give the remaining partner

extra grace to raise the children.

~

When my father and my mother forsake me,
then the LORD will take care of me.

Our children should be able to

look to us as examples of godly living.

~

*Listen to Me, you who follow after righteousness.... Look
to Abraham your father, and to Sarah who bore you.*

ISAIAH 51:1, 2

$\mathcal{J}$esus took time for little children.

How much time do we spend with them?

~

But Jesus said, "Let the little
children come to Me, and do not forbid them;
for of such is the kingdom of heaven."

$\mathcal{W}$e must have the moral courage

to stop inappropriate behavior

in our children's lives.

~

*For I have told him that I will
judge his house forever for the iniquity which
he knows, because his sons made themselves
vile, and he did not restrain them.*

1 SAMUEL 3:13

$\mathcal{G}$od loves your kids and

has a wonderful plan for their lives.

~

For whom He foreknew, He also predestined to be
conformed to the image of His Son, that He might be
the firstborn among many brethren.

ROMANS 8:29

$\mathscr{Y}$our kids are going to imitate
you. Let them see Jesus in your life.

~

Imitate me, just as I also imitate Christ.

1 CORINTHIANS 11:1

God never gives up on your
children, and neither should you.

~

*Being confident of this very thing, that He
who has begun a good work in you will complete
it until the day of Jesus Christ.*

PHILIPPIANS 1:6

$\mathcal{O}$ne of the most important lessons we can teach our children is that they must assume responsibility for their own actions.

~

So then each of us shall give account of himself to God.

ROMANS 14:12

$\mathcal{D}$on't let your mate or your kids go to sleep with unresolved conflicts between you.

~

Be angry, and do not sin: do not let the
sun go down on your wrath.

EPHESIANS 4:26

$\mathcal{G}$od wants to give us the wisdom we need as parents. All we have to do is ask Him for it.

~

If any of you lacks wisdom, let him ask of God,
who gives to all liberally and without reproach,
and it will be given to him.

JAMES 1:5

$\mathcal{D}$iscipline, properly administered
with love, helps a child to mature.

~

*Foolishness is bound up in the heart of a child; the
rod of correction will drive it far from him.*

PROVERBS 22:15

When a husband honors his wife, the children see a wonderful example to follow.

~

Her children rise up and call her blessed; her husband also, and he praises her.

PROVERBS 31:28

$\mathcal{T}$ake heart, parents! Some day
your kids will grow up and out of those
behaviors that irritate you.

~

*When I was a child, I spoke as a child, I understood
as a child, I thought as a child: but when I became a
man, I put away childish things.*

1 CORINTHIANS 13:11

Children will be content when they willingly obey their parents and God.

~

All your children shall be taught by the LORD, and great shall be the peace of your children.

ISAIAH 54:13

$\mathcal{A}$ father should never allow his children to speak disrespectfully to their mother.

~

For Moses said, "Honor your father and your mother";
and, "He who curses father or mother,
let him be put to death."

MARK 7:10

When we see our children
walking with God, our hearts are
filled with joy and gratitude.

~

*My son, if your heart is wise, my heart
will rejoice—indeed, I myself.*

PROVERBS 23:15

43

When your children see how
much you enjoy life as a Christian, it will
be harder for the world to convince them
they are missing out.

~

*I have come that they may have life, and that
they may have it more abundantly.*

JOHN 10:10

$\mathcal{F}$athers, you have an awesome
responsibility as the head of your home.
Some day you will give an account for how
you handled that responsibility.

~

For the husband is head of the wife, as also
Christ is head of the church.

EPHESIANS 5:23

$\mathcal{I}$t is hard on Christian parents when their children rebel and turn away from God. But He is faithful, even when our hearts are broken.

~

But his sons did not walk in his ways; they turned aside after dishonest gain, took bribes, and perverted justice.

1 SAMUEL 8:3

A wise, loving word from Mom
can lift the burdens of the world from
her children's shoulders.

~

She opens her mouth with wisdom,
and on her tongue is the law of kindness.

PROVERBS 31:26

$\mathcal{W}$hen our children are truly sorry,

it is time to hug them and forgive them.

~

And he arose and came to his father.
But when he was still a great way off,
his father saw him and had compassion,
and ran and fell on his neck and kissed him.

LUKE 15:20

48

$\mathcal{W}$hen you don't make your kids
responsible for their behavior, you are
asking for heartache.

~

*And his father had not rebuked him at any time
by saying, "Why have you done so?"*

1 KINGS 1:6

$\mathcal{P}$raying for your children

is the greatest thing you can do

for them. Be willing to leave

the results up to God.

~

David therefore pleaded with God
for the child, and David fasted and went
in and lay all night on the ground.

2 SAMUEL 12:16

$\mathcal{G}$od the Father praised

His Son. Surely it is a good thing

for us to praise our children.

~

*And suddenly a voice came from
heaven, saying, "This is My beloved Son,
in whom I am well pleased."*

MATTHEW 3:17

$\mathcal{W}$e should desire and pray for God's will
in our children's lives—but not manipulate
the circumstances to achieve it.

~

Then the mother of Zebedee's sons came to [Jesus] with
her sons, kneeling down and asking something from Him.
And He said to her, "What do you wish?" She said to Him, "Grant
that these two sons of mine may sit, one on Your right hand
and the other on the left, in Your kingdom."

MATTHEW 20:20, 21

$\mathcal{A}$ll children are a gift from God—
and they should be treasured as such.

~

Behold, children are a heritage from the LORD,
the fruit of the womb is a reward.

PSALM 127:3

Husbands should not only honor
their wives but protect them from anything or
anyone who might harm them.

~

Husbands, likewise, dwell with them with
understanding, giving honor to the wife, as to the weaker
vessel, and as being heirs together of the grace of life,
that your prayers may not be hindered.

1 Peter 3:7

54

$\mathscr{A}$ mother's love is stronger than steel. No force on earth can sever it.

～

Then the woman whose son was living spoke to the king, for she yearned with compassion for her son; and she said, "O my lord, give her the living child, and by no means kill him!"

1 KINGS 3:26

$\mathcal{G}$enuine love between a husband
and wife is priceless. Children will
thrive in a loving home.

~

*Many waters cannot quench love, nor can the floods
drown it. If a man would give for love all the wealth of
his house, it would be utterly despised.*

SONG OF SOLOMON 8:7

*W*hat greater security could we give our children than to assure them that we, like God, will always be there for them?

~

*In the fear of the L*ORD *there is strong confidence, and His children will have a place of refuge.*

PROVERBS 14:26

Since we live in a materialistic society,
we must teach our children that serving God
is the real meaning of success.

~

Now godliness with contentment is great gain.

1 TIMOTHY 6:6

$\mathcal{O}$ur children will have self-esteem
if they see themselves as the King's kids.
Their identity lies in their relationship to
the great God of the universe.

~

For in him we live and move and have our being, ...

ACTS 17:28

$\mathcal{M}$om and Dad should always

stand together—no matter what the issue.

~

Fulfill my joy by being
like-minded, having the same love,
being of one accord, of one mind.

PHILIPPIANS 2:2

$\mathcal{W}$e are good forgetters,

and that is why we need to keep

reminding ourselves and our children

of God's commandments.

~

Only take heed to yourself, and diligently
keep yourself, lest you forget the things your
eyes have seen, and lest they depart from your
heart all the days of your life. And teach
them to your children and your grandchildren.

DEUTERONOMY 4:9

*P*utting a stumbling block to faith in the
path of a child is a serious matter to God,
and a sobering reminder to us.

~

*It would be better for him if a millstone were hung
around his neck, and he were thrown into the sea, than
that he should offend one of these little ones.*

LUKE 17:2

When we dedicate our children to God, we are offering them for His service— after all, they belong to Him.

~

Then she made a vow and said, "O LORD of hosts, if You will indeed look on the affliction of Your maidservant and remember me, and not forget Your maidservant, but will give Your maidservant a male child, then I will give him to the LORD all the days of his life."

1 SAMUEL 1:11

When we teach our children the importance of living a pure life, we must remind them that it is not their body that is involved—they belong to God.

Do you not know that your body is the temple of the Holy Spirit who is in you, whom you have from God, and you are not your own?

1 CORINTHIANS 6:19

$\mathcal{D}$on't give up hope! God will use even the tough experiences of life to build your child's character, as well as your own.

~

And not only that, but we also glory in tribulations, knowing that tribulation produces perseverance; and perseverance, character; and character, hope.

ROMANS 5:3-4

Of all the reasons we could

give our kids for obeying us, the best

one is that it pleases God.

~

Children, obey your parents in all things,
for this is well pleasing to the Lord.

COLOSSIANS 3:20

$\mathcal{G}$od is specific in His expectations
of us, and we should be just as specific
with our children.

~

*But fornication and all uncleanness or covetousness,
let it not even be named among you, as is fitting for
saints; neither filthiness, nor foolish talking, nor coarse
jesting, which are not fitting, but rather giving of thanks.*

EPHESIANS 5:3-4

$\mathcal{A}$s Christian parents, we must teach our children to respect and obey the laws of the land, and all other authority.

~

Let every soul be subject to the governing authorities. For there is no authority except from God, and the authorities that exist are appointed by God. Therefore whoever resists the authority resists the ordinance of God.

ROMANS 13:1-2

$\mathcal{T}$here is no more important spiritual and practical lesson we can teach our children than the principle of sowing and reaping. Choices always have consequences.

~

Do not be deceived, God is not mocked; for whatever a man sows, that he will also reap.

GALATIANS 6:7

$\mathcal{A}$s Christian parents, we
should always make it our aim to
live upright lives. Our reputation
will be something our children
can live up to—but not live down.

~

*The righteous man walks in his integrity; his
children are blessed after him.*

PROVERBS 20:7

$\mathcal{I}$n a world hostile to
Christian values, we need to prepare
our children to live wisely.

~

*See then that you walk circumspectly,
not as fools but as wise, redeeming the time,
because the days are evil.*

EPHESIANS 5:15-16

The image of God our children have is often filtered through the image of Him they see in us. We must give them a clear image!

~

So God created man in His own image; in the image of God He created him; male and female He created them.

GENESIS 1:27

The image of God our children have is often filtered through the image of Him they see in us. We must give them a clear image!

~

So God created man in His own image; in the image of God He created him; male and female He created them.

GENESIS 1:27

Children are not born with a knowledge of God's Word. They must be *taught* God's will and God's ways.

~

And that their children, who have not known it, may hear and learn to fear the LORD your God as long as you live in the land which you cross the Jordan to possess.

DEUTERONOMY 31:13

$\mathcal{W}$e all need acceptance. God gives it to us, and we need to give it to our children.

~

*I will be a Father to you, and you shall be My sons and daughters, says the L*ORD *Almighty.*

2 CORINTHIANS 6:18

$\mathscr{W}$e need to teach our children that when life gets rough and we do not see God's footsteps walking beside us, it may be because He is carrying us at that time, in that situation.

~

And in the wilderness where you saw how the LORD your God carried you, as a man carries his son, in all the way that you went until you came to this place.

DEUTERONOMY 1:31

Raising your children well without
God is not only difficult, it is impossible.

~

Unless the LORD builds the house, they labor
in vain who build it; unless the LORD guards the city,
the watchman stays awake in vain.

PSALM 127:1

As parents, we hurt or heal more
with our words than with anything else.

~

Set a guard, O Lord, over my mouth; keep
watch over the door of my lips.

PSALM 141:3

It takes a lot of love to
produce harmony in the home.

~

*Behold, how good and how pleasant it is for
brethren to dwell together in unity!*

PSALM 133:1

God adopted us into His family because
He wanted us. Our children, whether natural
or adopted, should feel equally wanted.

~

Having predestined us to adoption as sons by
Jesus Christ to Himself according to the good
pleasure of His will.

EPHESIANS 1:5

$\mathcal{K}$nowing what God expects

of us as spouses and parents, and even

wanting to do it, is not enough.

We must set about *doing* it!

~

*Therefore let us pursue the things
which make for peace and the things by
which one may edify another.*

ROMANS 14:19

$\mathcal{T}$here is no greater reward for parents

than to see their children come to know

Christ and grow in their faith.

~

I have no greater joy than to hear that
my children walk in truth.

3 JOHN 4

$\mathcal{I}$t is important that our children learn
early in life about the faithfulness of God
in meeting all of our needs.

~

*The young lions lack and suffer hunger; but those who
seek the LORD shall not lack any good thing.*

PSALM 34:10

82

$\mathcal{B}$efore our children go to sleep,
we should pray with them that God
will guard their thoughts and keep their
minds open to His instruction.

~

I will bless the LORD who has given me counsel; my heart
also instructs me in the night seasons.

PSALM 16:7

The way we talk to each other at home is a pretty good test of the health of our family life. We need to bless each other with our tongues!

~

Pleasant words are like a honeycomb, sweetness to the soul and health to the bones.

$\mathcal{F}$ar more important than popularity is respect. Respect comes from being a person of integrity. These values may not be what our children see and hear daily in the world, so we must teach them in our homes.

~

A good name is to be chosen rather than great riches, loving favor rather than silver and gold.

PROVERBS 22:1

The healthiest thing in the world would be for our children to become godly individualists who challenge those around them to yield to God's will instead of the world's.

~

And do not be conformed to this world, but be transformed by the renewing of your mind, that you may prove what is that good and acceptable and perfect will of God.

ROMANS 12:2

Children will become what their minds dwell upon. Provide them with all the good Christian literature and music you can acquire.

~

Finally, brethren, whatever things are true, whatever things are noble, whatever things are just, whatever things are pure, whatever things are lovely, whatever things are of good report, if there is any virtue and if there is anything praiseworthy— meditate on these things.

PHILIPPIANS 4:8

*I*n this world, the only safe place to be is in the center of God's revealed will. Our children need to be constantly reminded that God loves them, and so do we.

~

You are my hiding place; You shall preserve me from trouble; You shall surround me with songs of deliverance.

PSALM 32:7

$\mathcal{I}$f we say we are dissatisfied with what we have, we may be sending an unintended message to our children that we are unhappy with what God has provided for our family.

~

Let your conduct be without covetousness; be content with such things as you have. For He Himself has said, "I will never leave you nor forsake you."

HEBREWS 13:5

Children have problems
too. They need your listening
ear and sympathetic heart.

~

Bear one another's burdens,
and so fulfill the law of Christ.

GALATIANS 6:2

*T*here is no such thing as
a white lie. A lie is a lie, and your
children need to see you as a fierce
champion of the truth.

~

*Lying lips are an abomination
to the LORD, but those who deal
truthfully are His delight.*

PROVERBS 12:22

Dad, Mom, and the kids all have an essential part to play in the life of a family. The only way each individual can grow is if everyone does his or her part.

~

For as the body is one and has many members,
but all the members of that one body, being many,
are one body, so also is Christ.

1 CORINTHIANS 12:12

No one is immune from depression, even children. Everyone needs to be told they are valued, and that they are valuable. Jesus died to show us that.

~

Anxiety in the heart of man causes depression,
but a good word makes it glad.

PROVERBS 12:25

*E*ither God's Word will keep our
children from sin, or sin will keep our
children from God's Word.

~

How can a young man cleanse his way?
By taking heed according to Your word.

PSALM 119:9

Conflicts arise when our egos get in the way.
Mom and Dad can show the right way to live
by putting each other first.

~

Let nothing be done through selfish ambition or conceit,
but in lowliness of mind let each esteem others
better than himself.

<small>PHILIPPIANS 2:3</small>

$\mathcal{N}$othing clears the air so quickly as confessing that it was your fault and then seeking the other person's forgiveness. Try it on your kids and see what happens.

~

Confess your trespasses to one another,
and pray for one another.

JAMES 5:16

Teach your children an attitude of gratitude.
It keeps their eyes focused on the Giver.

~

Giving thanks always for all things to God the Father
in the name of our Lord Jesus Christ.

EPHESIANS 5:20

One of the best forms of spiritual training for your children is learning Bible verses. Start by teaching them at home and then seek a church that teaches children to love God's Word.

Your word I have hidden in my heart,
that I might not sin against You.

PSALM 119:11

$\mathcal{P}$arents, if you focus on your own inadequacy, you will never be at peace. If you concentrate on Jesus' all-sufficiency, your minds can rest because your confidence will be in Him.

You will keep him in perfect peace,
whose mind is stayed on You.

ISAIAH 26:3

$\mathcal{W}$e will never be the husband
or wife we should be unless we leave
our hang-ups with parents behind. If
we don't, we may ruin our marriages and
transfer our hang-ups to our kids.

~

*Therefore a man shall leave his father
and mother and be joined to his wife, and
they shall become one flesh.*

GENESIS 2:24

$\mathcal{W}$e must learn from past mistakes,
but not wallow in them. Don't keep
reminding your spouse or your kids of
things that have been settled
between you. Move on.

~

*One thing I do, forgetting those things which
are behind and reaching forward to those things
which are ahead, I press toward the goal for the prize
of the upward call of God in Christ Jesus.*

PHILIPPIANS 3:13-14

$\mathcal{Y}$ou wanted to say the right things
to your kids, but your words came out harsh
again. Consciously submit your heart and your
tongue to God's control, and ask
forgiveness from your kids.

~

*The preparations of the heart belong to man, but the
answer of the tongue is from the LORD.*

PROVERBS 16:1

The purpose of discipline is to break
the child's self-will, not his or her spirit.

~

Fathers, do not provoke your children,
lest they become discouraged.

COLOSSIANS 3:21

*I*n communicating with one another, God expects us to be honest *and* loving. Problems arise when we are honest but not loving.

~

But speaking the truth in love, [we] may grow up in all things into Him who is the head—Christ.

EPHESIANS 4:15

Sometimes our children have to learn the hard way. How much better off they would be if they had listened to us in the first place.

~

A fool despises his father's instruction, but he who receives correction is prudent.

PROVERBS 15:5

The Holy Spirit can speak to our children just as He can to us. We need to show respect for their spiritual insights.

~

And it shall come to pass afterward that I will pour out My Spirit on all flesh; your sons and your daughters shall prophesy, your old men shall dream dreams, your young men shall see visions.

JOEL 2:28

*J*ust as God listens to us,

so we need to take the time to listen—

really listen—to our kids.

~

I love the Lord, *because He has heard my voice and my*
supplications. Because He has inclined His ear to me,
therefore I will call upon Him as long as I live.

Psalm 116:1-2

$\mathcal{I}$f we listen to our spouses with our hearts as well as our ears, we will be able to respond correctly to what they are saying.

~

He who answers a matter before he hears it,
it is folly and shame to him.

PROVERBS 18:13

$\mathcal{O}$ur children are often aggressive on
the outside because a war is going on inside.

~

Where do wars and fights come from among you?
Do they not come from your desires for pleasure that
war in your members?

JAMES 4:1

$\mathcal{A}$ godly wife is the best thing
that will ever happen to a husband.

~

He who finds a wife finds a good thing,
and obtains favor from the LORD.

PROVERBS 18:22

The one thing you *can* control

in a family conflict is yourself.

~

If it is possible, as much as depends on you,
live peaceably with all men.

ROMANS 12:18

$\mathcal{M}$ature, godly love between a husband and wife results in each one trying to outdo the other in meeting the other's needs.

~

So husbands ought to love their own wives as their own bodies; he who loves his wife loves himself.

<small>EPHESIANS 5:28</small>

The Spirit-filled family is one that practices mutual submission in love.

~

Be filled with the Spirit, . . . submitting to one another in the fear of God.

EPHESIANS 5:18, 21

$\mathcal{P}$arents must pull together,

or their children will be torn apart.

~

Endeavoring to keep the unity of the
Spirit in the bond of peace.

$\mathcal{G}$od wants you and your family
to be a testimony before the church and
a witness to the world.

~

*Here am I and the children whom the LORD has
given me! We are for signs and wonders in
Israel from the LORD of hosts.*

ISAIAH 8:18

A love for God's Word is an acquired taste. As parents, we have the opportunity to whet our children's appetites.

~

As newborn babes, desire the pure milk of the word, that you may grow thereby.

1 PETER 2:2

The Bible is a complete manual for raising children. Trying to raise them without it is like trying to build a house without blueprints.

~

All Scripture is given by inspiration of God, and is profitable for doctrine, for reproof, for correction, for instruction in righteousness, ...

2 TIMOTHY 3:16

$\mathcal{E}$very home needs a family altar: a time and a place where the parents teach their children how to worship God.

~

Come, you children, listen to me; I will teach you the fear of the LORD.

PSALM 34:11

The golden years provide a golden opportunity for grandparents to impart a lifetime of wisdom to their grandchildren.

~

Now also when I am old and grayheaded, O God, do not forsake me; until I declare Your strength to this generation, Your power to everyone who is to come.

PSALM 71:18

$\mathscr{P}$arents have no greater
responsibility than to help build the
character of their children.

~

Giving all diligence, add to your faith virtue,
to virtue knowledge, to knowledge self-control,
to self-control perseverance, to perseverance godliness,
to godliness brotherly kindness, and to
brotherly kindness love.

2 PETER 1:5-7

$\mathcal{A}$s parents, we have the unique
privilege of helping our children to
discover their spiritual gifts.

~

There are diversities of gifts, but the same Spirit.

1 CORINTHIANS 12:4

$\mathcal{T}$he value of knowing Jesus when
you are a young person is that you have a
whole lifetime to live for Him.

~

*For You are my hope, O Lord GOD, You are
my trust from my youth.*

PSALM 71:5

$\mathcal{G}$od has designed it so that husbands and wives need each other. Neither can play their God-given role without the other.

~

Nevertheless, neither is man independent of woman, nor woman independent of man, in the Lord.

1 CORINTHIANS 11:11

$\mathcal{W}$e must impress upon our children
that they are indeed responsible for one
another's spiritual welfare.

~

Then the LORD said to Cain, "Where is Abel your brother?"

GENESIS 4:9

124

$\mathcal{G}$od understands the broken heart
of a parent whose child has wandered.

~

*Hear, O heavens, and give ear, O earth! For the LORD
has spoken:"I have nourished and brought up children,
and they have rebelled against Me."*

ISAIAH 1:2

*I*f our children commit themselves to living holy lives, we as parents should do everything in our power to support them in their resolve.

~

But Daniel purposed in his heart that he would not defile himself with the portion of the king's delicacies, nor with the wine which he drank.

DANIEL 1:8

Once our children realize that the greatest power in the universe—God Himself—dwells within them, they should never feel inferior or intimidated again.

~

You are of God, little children, and have overcome them, because He who is in you is greater than he who is in the world.

1 JOHN 4:4

$\mathcal{W}$e need to lead our family in prayer for
revival. When the Holy Spirit produces a revival,
it will touch every member of the family.

~

*Now while Ezra was praying, and while he was confessing,
weeping, and bowing down before the house of God, a
very large assembly of men, women, and children gathered
to him from Israel; for the people wept very bitterly.*

EZRA 10:1

$\mathcal{G}$od has modeled for us the perfect balance between justice and mercy. That should be the ideal of our homes as well.

~

Righteousness and justice are the foundation of Your throne; mercy and truth go before Your face.

PSALM 89:14

$\mathcal{W}$hen Christian families take a stand for God, the ripple effect can touch the entire nation.

~

Choose for yourselves this day whom you will serve, ... But as for me and my house, we will serve the LORD.

JOSHUA 24:15

*L*et our children see us as
men and women of consistent prayer.

~

*The effective, fervent prayer of a
righteous man avails much.*

JAMES 5:16

$\mathcal{P}$arenting is the work of God. Even if we faint or feel like giving up, He has guaranteed that our efforts will bear fruit in eternity.

~

Therefore, my beloved brethren, be steadfast, immovable, always abounding in the work of the Lord, knowing that your labor is not in vain in the Lord.

1 CORINTHIANS 15:58

$\mathcal{I}$f children find encouragement in the home,

they will not have to seek it elsewhere.

~

Therefore comfort each other and edify one another,
just as you also are doing.

1 THESSALONIANS 5:11

One of the most important things
Mom and Dad can do for their children at
school is to pray for them.

~

*Again I say to you that if two of you agree on earth
concerning anything that they ask, it will be done for
them by My Father in heaven.*

MATTHEW 18:19

$\mathcal{O}$ur children can save themselves a lot of grief if they will but heed the instruction and follow the example of godly parents.

~

The things which you learned and received and heard and saw in me, these do, and the God of peace will be with you.

PHILIPPIANS 4:9

Jesus wraps it all up for us when He commands us to love one another. A cord of three strands—Dad, Mom, and child—is hard to break.

~

A new commandment I give to you, that you love one another; as I have loved you, that you also love one another.

JOHN 13:34